MW01223909

Amigurumi Sea Creatures

Amigurumi Crochet Sea Creature Animal Toy Patterns

Copyright © 2020

All rights reserved.

DEDICATION

The author and publisher have provided this e-book to you for your personal use only. You may not make this e-book publicly available in any way. Copyright infringement is against the law. If you believe the copy of this e-book you are reading infringes on the author's copyright, please notify the publisher at: https://us.macmillan.com/piracy

Contents

Baby Humpback Crochet Whale

SUPPLIES

2 balls: Lion Brand Vanna's Choice in Denim Mist (85g/3oz, 145yds/133m, 4 Medium)

1 ball: Lion Brand Vanna's Choice in Silver Blue (100g/3.5ox, 170yds/156m, 4 Medium)

1 Clover USA crochet hook G/4.00mm*

9mm safety eyes

stitch markers

polyfill stuffing

scissors

tapestry needle

ABBREVIATIONS

sl st – slip stitch

ch – chain stitch

hdc – half double crochet

dc – double crochet

sc2tog – single crochet decrease: Insert hook into front loop of next st. Without yarning over, insert hook into front loop of next st. Yarn over. Pull through 2 loops on hook. Yarn over, pull through remaining loop on hook.

PATTERN NOTES

The Whale Top uses Denim Mist – Color A. The Whale Bottom uses Silver Blue – Color B. Make 4 Whale Fins, two using Color A, and two using Color B.

Gauge = 18 stitches and 18 rows in 4 inches.

Overall size = approximately 17 inches long and 13 inches from fin tip to fin tip.

Turn at the end of each Row.

Most rows are the reflected over the halfway point. In other words, they are palindromes! The exceptions are the single decrease stitches.

Anytime it's written just X sc, it means work 1 sc in each of next X stitches. Eg. "6 sc, 2 sc in next 2 st, 6 sc" = Work 1 sc in each of next 6 st, 2 sc in each of next 2 st, 1 sc in each of next 6 st.

Rows 20-21: the last stitch is the 2nd chain of the 'Ch 2' from the previous row.

"Row 37: Ch 1. Work 1 sc, 1 sc2tog, 20 sc, 1 sc2tog, 20 sc, 1 sc2tog, 1 sc. (45)" = Work 1 sc in first st. Work the next 2 st together into 1 sc. Work 1 sc in each of the next 20 st. Work the next 2 st together into 1 sc. Work 1 sc in each of the next 20 st. Work the next 2 st together into 1 sc. Work 1 sc in the last st. => You start with 48 stitches in the previous row, and you are decreasing into 45 stitches.

Row 49 is where the work is folded to create the fin. The previous row is 38 stitches. Fold your work in half, so there's 19 stitches in each half. Work 1 sc in first st. Work the next 2 st together into 1 sc. Work 1 sc in each of next 12 st (all as normal). With the work folded in half, you should see 4 stitches left before the turn. Work 1 sc in each of those next 4 st, but work through all 4 loops to secure them together. You've now worked through 19 stitches and it looks like it's the end of the "row". Ch 1 and turn. Work 1 sl st into each of the previous 4 sc that you created. Now, there should be 15 unworked stitches left in the row. Work 1 sc in each of 12 st (normal 2 loops only at this point). Work the next 2 st together into 1 sc. Work 1 sc in last st.

Rows 74-76: Keep your slip stitches fairly loose so that it's easier to work a new row of slip stitches into slip stitches. Otherwise, these 4 stitches get a bit tricky. This is to create the little divot in the tail.

Whale assembly uses a combination of slip stitches and the mattress stitch.

Below instructions are to attach the fins by working them directly into the mattress stitch while joining the whale together. Alternatively, attach the fins by sewing them directly onto the finished whale.

PATTERN

WHALE TOP – Using Color A

Row 1: Chain 11.

Row 2: Starting from the second chain from hook, work 1 sc in each st across. (10)

Row 3: Ch 1. Work 1 sc in each st across. (10)

Row 4: Ch 1. Work 2 sc in first st, 3 sc, 2 sc in next 2 st, 3 sc, 2 sc in last st. (14)

Row 5: Ch 1. Work 1 sc in each st across. (14)

Row 6: Ch 1. Work 6 sc, 2 sc in next 2 st, 6 sc. (16)

Row 7: Ch 1. Work 7 sc, 2 sc in next 2 st, 7 sc. (18)

Row 8: Ch 1. Work 8 sc, 2 sc in next 2 st, 8 sc. (20)

Row 9-11: Ch 1. Work 1 sc in each st across. (20)

Row 12: Ch 1. Work 9 sc, 2 sc in next 2 st, 9 sc. (22)

Row 13: Ch 1. Work 2 sc in first st, 20 sc, 2 sc in last st. (24)

Row 14: Ch 1. Work 2 sc in first st, 10 sc, 2 sc in next 2 st, 10 sc, 2 sc in last st. (28)

Row 15: Ch 1. Work 1 sc in each st across (28)

Row 16: Ch 1. Work 2 sc in first st, 26 sc, 2sc in last st. (30)

Row 17: Ch 1. Work 2 sc in first st, 13 sc, 2 sc in next 2 st, 13 sc, 2 sc in last st. (34)

Row 18: Ch 1. Work 2 sc in first st, 32 sc, 2 sc in last st. (36)

Row 19: Ch 2 – counts as stitch. Work 1 hdc in first st, 34 sc, 2 hdc in last st. (38)

Row 20: Ch 2 – counts as stitch. Work 1 hdc in first st, 36 sc, 2 hdc in last st. (40)

Row 21: Ch 1. Work 2 sc in first st, 38 sc, 2 sc in last st. (42)

Row 22: Ch 1. Work 20 sc, 2 sc in next 2 st, 20 sc. (44)

Row 23-24: Ch 1. Work 1 sc in each st across. (44)

Row 25: Ch 1. Work 2 sc in first st, 42 sc, 2 sc in last st. (46)

Row 26: Ch 1. Work 1 sc in each st across. (46)

Row 27: Ch 1. Work 2 sc in first st, 44 sc, 2 sc in last st. (48)

Row 28-36: Ch 1. Work 1 sc in each st across. (48)

Row 37: Ch 1. Work 1 sc in first st, 1 sc2tog, 20 sc, 1 sc2tog, 20 sc, 1 sc2tog, 1 sc in last st. (45)

Row 38: Ch 1. Work 1 sc in each st across. (45)

Row 39: Ch 1. Work 1 sc in first st, 1 sc2tog, 18 sc, 1 sc2tog, 19 sc, 1 sc2tog, 1 sc in last st. (42)

Row 40: Ch 1. Work 1 sc in each st across. (42)

Row 41: Ch 1. Work 1 sc, 1 sc2tog, 36 sc, 1 sc2tog, 1 sc. (40)

Row 42: Ch 1. Work 1 sc in each st across. (40)

Row 43: Ch 1. Work 1 sc in first st, 1 sc2tog, 16 sc, 2 sc in next 2 st, 16 sc, 1 sc2tog, 1 sc in last st. (40) This is the start of the back fin.

Row 44: Ch 1. Work 19 sc, 2 sc in next 2 st, 19 sc. (42)

Row 45: Ch 1. Work 1 sc in first st, 1 sc2tog, 36 sc, 1 sc2tog, 1 sc in last st. (40)

Row 46-47: Repeat Rows 44-45.

Row 48: Ch 1. Work 1 sc in first st, 1 sc2tog, 34 sc, 1 sc2tog, 1 sc in last st. (38)

Row 49: Ch 1. Work 1 sc in first st, 1 sc2tog, 12 sc. Fold your work in half and pinch the center 8 stitches together. Work 1 sc in each of next 4 st, through all 4 loops. Ch 1, turn. Work 1 sl st in each of next 4 st. Work 12 sc, 1 sc2tog, 1 sc in last st. (36) This is the end of the back fin. See Pattern Notes for more details on this row.

Row 50: Ch 1. Work 1 sc in each st across. (28)

Row 51: Ch 1. Work 1 sc in first st, 1 sc2tog, 10 sc, 1 sc2tog, 10 sc, 1 sc2tog, 1 sc in last st. (25)

Row 52: Ch 1. Work 1 sc in each st across. (25)

Row 53: Ch 1. Work 1 sc in first st, 1 sc2tog, 8 sc, 1 sc2tog, 9 sc, 1 sc2tog, 1 sc in last st. (22)

Row 54: Ch 1. Work 1 sc in each st across. (22)

Row 55: Ch 1. Work 1 sc in first st, 1 sc2tog, 16 sc, 1 sc2tog, 1 sc in last st. (20)

Row 56: Ch 1. Work 1 sc in each st across. (20)

Row 57: Ch 1. Work 1 sc in first st, 1 sc2tog, 6 sc, 1 sc2tog, 6 sc, 1 sc2tog, 1 sc in last st. (17)

Row 58: Ch 1. Work 1 sc in each st across. (17)

Row 59: Ch 1. Work 1 sc in first st, 1 sc2tog, 4 sc, 1 sc2tog, 5 sc, 1 sc2tog, 1 sc in last st. (14)

Row 60: Ch 1. Work 1 sc in each st across. (14)

Row 61: Ch 1. Work 1 sc in first st, 1 sc2tog, 3 sc, 1 sc2tog, 3 sc, 1 sc2tog, 1 sc in last st. (11)

Row 62: Ch 1. Work 1 sc in each st across. (11)

Row 63: Ch 1. Work 1 sc in first st, 1 sc2tog, 1 sc, 1 sc2tog, 2 sc, 1 sc2tog, 1 sc in last st. (8)

Row 64: Ch 1. Work 1 sc in each st across. (8)

Row 65: Ch 1. Work 1 sc in first st, 1 sc2tog, 2 sc, 1 sc2tog, 1 sc in last st. (6)

Row 66: Ch 1. Work 1 sc in each st across. (6)

START OF TAIL

Row 67: Ch 1. Work 2 sc in first st, 4 sc, 2 sc in last st. (8)

Row 68: Ch 1. Work 2 sc in first st, 6 sc, 2 sc in last st. (10)

Row 69: Ch 1. Work 2 sc in first st, 8 sc, 2 sc in last st. (12)

Row 70: Ch 1. Work 2 sc in first st, 10 sc, 2 sc in last st. (14)

Row 71: Ch 1. Work 2 sc in first st, 12 sc, 2 sc in last st. (16)

Row 72: Ch 2 – counts as 1 hdc st. Work 1 hdc in first st, 14 sc, 2 hdc in last st. (18)

Row 73: Ch 3 – counts as 1 dc st. Work 1 dc in first st, 16 sc, 2 dc in last st. (20)

Row 74: Ch 3 – counts as 1 dc st. Work 1 dc in first st, 7 hdc, 4 sl st, 7 hdc, 2 dc in last st. (22)

Row 75: Ch 3 – counts as 1 dc st. Work 1 dc in first st, 8 hdc, 4 sl st, 8 hdc, 2 dc in last st. (22)

Row 76: Ch 3 – counts as 1 dc st. Work 1 dc in first st, 9 hdc, 4 sl st, 9 hdc, 2 dc in last st. (22)

Fasten off, weave in ends.

WHALE BOTTOM – Using Color B

Row 1: Chain 17.

Row 2: Starting from the second chain from hook, work 7 sc, 2 sc in next 2 st, 7 sc. (18)

Row 3: Ch 1. Work 8 sc, 2 sc in next 2 st, 8 sc. (20)

Row 4: Ch 1. Work 1 sc, 1 sc2tog, 5 sc, 1 hdc, 2 dc in next 2 st, 1 hdc, 5 sc, 1 sc2tog, 1 sc st. (20)

Row 5: Ch 1. Work 8 sc, 2 hdc in next st, 2 dc in next 2 st, 2 hdc in next st, 8 sc. (24)

Row 6: Ch 1. Work 10 sc, 2 sc in next st, 2 hdc in next 2 st, 2 sc in next st, 10 sc. (28)

Row 7: Ch 1. Work 1 sc in each st across. (28)

Row 8: Ch 1. Work 13 sc, 2 sc in next 2 st, 13 sc. (30)

Row 9: Ch 1. Work 14 sc, 2 sc in next 2 st, 14 sc. (32)

Row 10: Ch 1. Work 1 sc in each st across. (32)

Row 11: Ch 1. Work 15 sc, 2 sc in next 2 st, 15 sc. (34)

Row 12: Ch 1. Work 16 sc, 2 sc in next 2 st, 16 sc. (36)

Row 13: Ch 1. Work 1 sc in first st, 1 sc2tog, 30 sc, 1 sc2tog, 1 sc in last st. (34)

Row 14: Ch 1. Work 1 sc in first st, 1 sc2tog, 13 sc, 2 sc in next 2 st, 13 sc, 1 sc2tog, 1 sc. (34)

Row 15: Ch 1. Work 1 sc in each st across. (34)

Row 16: Ch 1. Work 1 sc in first st, 1 sc2tog, 13 sc, 2 sc in next 2 st, 13 sc, 1 sc2tog, 1 sc. (34)

Row 17: Ch 1. Work 1 sc in first st, 1 sc2tog, 28 sc, 1 sc2tog, 1 sc in last st. (32)

Row 18: Ch 1. Work 1 sc in first st, 1 sc2tog, 12 sc, 2 sc in next 2 st, 12 sc, 1 sc2tog, 1 sc. (32)

Row 19: Ch 1. Work 2 sc2tog (over 4 st), 24 sc, 2 sc2tog (over 4 st). (28)

Row 20: Ch 1. Work 1 sc in each st across. (28)

Row 21: Ch 1. Work 1 sc in first st, 1 sc2tog, 22 sc, 1 sc2tog, 1 sc in last st. (26)

Row 22-24: Ch 1. Work 1 sc in each st across. (26)

Row 25: Ch 1. Work 1 sc in first st, 1 sc2tog, 20 sc, 1 sc2tog, 1 sc in last st. (24)

Row 26: Ch 1. Work 1 sc in each st across. (24)

Row 27: Ch 1. Work 1 sc in first st, 1 sc2tog, 18 sc, 1 sc2tog, 1 sc in last st. (22)

Row 28-36: Ch 1. Work 1 sc in each st across. (22)

Row 37: Ch 1. Work 2 sc in first st, 9 sc, 1 sc2tog, 9 sc, 2 sc in last st. (23)

Row 38: Ch 1. Work 11 sc, 1 sc2tog, 10 sc. (22)

Row 39: Ch 1. Work 2 sc in first st, 8 sc, 2 sc2tog, 8 sc, 2 sc in last st. (22)

Row 40: Ch 1. Work 1 sc in each st across. (22)

Row 41-42: Repeat Rows 39-40. (22)

Row 43: Ch 1. Work 2 sc in first st, 8 sc, 2 sc2tog, 8 sc, 2 sc in last st. (22)

Row 44: Ch 1. Work 9 sc, 2 sc2tog, 9 sc. (20)

Row 45: Ch 1. Work 2 sc in first st, 7 sc, 2 sc2tog, 7 sc, 2 sc in last st. (20)

Row 46: Ch 1. Work 8 sc, 2 sc2tog, 8 sc. (18)

Row 47: Ch 1. Work 2 sc in first st, 6 sc, 2 sc2tog, 6 sc, 2 sc in last st. (18)

Row 48: Ch 1. Work 7 sc, 2 sc2tog, 7 sc. (16)

Row 49: Ch 1. Work 2 sc in first st, 5 sc, 2 sc2tog, 5 sc, 2 sc in last st. (16)

Row 50: Ch 1. Work 1 sc in each st across. (16)

Row 51: Ch 1. Work 2 sc in first st, 5 sc, 2 sc2tog, 5 sc, 2 sc in last st. (16)

Row 52: Ch 1. Work 6 sc, 2 sc2tog, 6 sc. (14)

Row 53: Ch 1. Work 2 sc in first st, 4 sc, 2 sc2tog, 4 sc, 2 sc in last st. (14)

Row 54: Ch 1. Work 1 sc in each st across. (14)

Row 55: Ch 1. Work 2 sc in first st, 4 sc, 2 sc2tog, 4 sc, 2 sc in last st. (14)

Row 56: Ch 1. Work 5 sc, 2 sc2tog, 5 sc. (12)

Row 57: Ch 1. Work 2 sc in first st, 3 sc, 2 sc2tog, 3 sc, 2 sc in last st. (12)

Row 58: Ch 1. Work 4 sc, 2 sc2tog, 4 sc. (10)

Row 59: Ch 1. Work 2 sc in first st, 2 sc, 2 sc2tog, 2 sc, 2 sc in last st. (10)

Row 60: Ch 1. Work 3 sc, 2 sc2tog, 3 sc. (8)

Row 61: Ch 1. Work 2 sc in first st, 1 sc, 2 sc2tog, 1 sc, 2 sc in last st. (8)

Row 62: Ch 1. Work 2 sc, 2 sc2tog, 2 sc. (6)

Row 63: Ch 1. Work 2 sc in first st, 2 sc2tog, 2 sc in last st. (6)

Row 64: Ch 1. Work 1 sc in each st across. (6)

Row 65-66: Repeat Rows 63-64.

START OF TAIL

Row 67: Ch 1. Work 2 sc in first st, 4 sc, 2 sc in last st. (8)

Row 68: Ch 1. Work 2 sc in first st, 6 sc, 2 sc in last st. (10)

Row 69: Ch 1. Work 2 sc in first st, 8 sc, 2 sc in last st. (12)

Row 70: Ch 1. Work 2 sc in first st, 10 sc, 2 sc in last st. (14)

Row 71: Ch 1. Work 2 sc in first st, 12 sc, 2 sc in last st. (16)

Row 72: Ch 2 – counts as 1 hdc st. Work 1 hdc in first st, 14 sc, 2 hdc in last st. (18)

Row 73: Ch 3 – counts as 1 dc st. Work 1 dc in first st, 16 sc, 2 dc in last st. (20)

Row 74: Ch 3 – counts as 1 dc st. Work 1 dc in first st, 7 hdc, 4 sl st, 7 hdc, 2 dc in last st. (22)

Row 75: Ch 3 – counts as 1 dc st. Work 1 dc in first st, 8 hdc, 4 sl st, 8 hdc, 2 dc in last st. (22)

Row 76: Ch 3 – counts as 1 dc st. Work 1 dc in first st, 9 hdc, 4 sl st, 9 hdc, 2 dc in last st. (22)

Fasten off, weave in ends.

WHALE FINS (Make 4 – 2 in each color)

Row 1: Ch 6.

Row 2: Starting from the second chain from hook, work 1 sc in each st across. (5)

Row 3: Ch 1. Work 1 sc in each st across. (5)

Row 4: Ch 1. Work 1 sc in each of next 4 st, 2 sc in last st. (6)

Row 5: Ch 1. Work 1 sc in each st across. (6)

Row 6: Ch 1. Work 1 sc in each of next 5 st, 2 sc in last st. (7)

Row 7-8: Ch 1. Work 1 sc in each st across. (7)

Row 9: Ch 1. Work 1 sc in first st, 1 sc2tog, 1 sc in each of next 4 st. (6)

Row 10: Ch 1. Work 1 sc in each st across. (6)

Row 11: Ch 1. Work 1 sc in first st, 1 sc2tog, 1 sc in each of next 3 st. (5)

Row 12-15: Ch 1. Work 1 sc in each st across. (5)

Row 16: Ch 1. Work 1 sc in first st, 1 sc2tog, 1 sc in each of next 2 st. (4)

Row 17-18: Ch 1. Work 1 sc in each st across. (4)

Row 19: Ch 1. Work 1 sc in each of next 2 st, 1 sc2tog. (3)

Row 20: Ch 1. Work 1 sc2tog, then sl st into last st. (2)

Fasten off and weave in ends.

ASSEMBLY

Attach safety eyes at approx. Row 21 on Whale Top, about 3 stitches from either edge.

On both Whale Top and Whale Bottom, fold Row 1 in half, sew together to form nose.

Fins:

Hold a Color A fin and a Color B fin together, edges lined up. Using Color A, insert hook through both fins (4 loops together), and attach yarn. Work slip stitches evenly around the fin. Join to first sl st.

Repeat for the other set of fins, making sure they are lined up opposite the first set so that the straight edge of both fins face forward.

Whale Body:

Holding the Top and Bottom tail fins together, attach yarn at Row 66 (right side while facing the whale). Work slip stitches evenly around the tail fin until Row 66, left side.

Cut the yarn, leaving approximately a 4 ft tail for joining the whale body.

Pull yarn through last slip stitch at Row 66 to secure.

Use the mattress stitch to join the Whale Top to Whale Bottom, edge to edge, working from the left side while facing the whale, around the front and down the right side of the whale. Make sure to line up the rows on both pieces. Having stitch markers in place helps a lot!

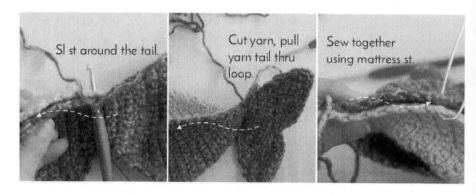

At Row 28 of left side, work the mattress stitch through the left fin to sew the fin directly into the body. Fin should be attached from approximately Row 28 to Row 24.

Continue joining the Whale Top to Whale Bottom around the front of the whale.

At Row 24 of right side, work the mattress stitch through the right fin to sew the fin directly into the body. Fin should be attached from approximately Row 24 to Row 28.

Continue joining the Whale Top to Whale Bottom, stopping to stuff the whale, until Row 66.

Sew into where the yarn was first attached. Secure tightly and fasten off. Weave in ends.

All done!

Naiad The Nudibranch

Abbreviation list

ch – chain

Sc – simple crochet

Dc – double crochet

Sl st – slip stitch

PATTERN

Main body – worked from top to bottom in the round

With MC

Ch 26 (starting chain + turning ch)

Round 1: Sc in the second ch from the hook, sc 24 (you should now be in your first ch), sc 3 more in your first ch. Sc 24 on the other side of your starting chain, sc 2 more in your last ch. You should have 4 sc at each end ch of your starting chain and 23 sc either part of your starting chain (see photo) – 54 st

Round 2: sc all around – 54 st

Round 3-5: Repeat round 2 – 54 st

Round 6: sc 24, *2 sc in next st* x 2, sc 25, 2sc in next st, 2 sc in next st, sc 1 – 58 st

Round 7-8: Repeat round 2 – 58 st

Round 9: sc 25, 2sc in next st, 2 sc in next st, sc 27, 2sc in next st, 2 sc in next st, sc 2 – 62 st

Join in CC1

Round 10: Ch3 (counts as the first dc), 2 dc more in the same st, 3dc in each st all around. sl st at the top of the first dc. Fasten off and weave in ends

Gills – at the back of the body

This part of the amigurumi is worked in the round. I used the MC but you can also use CC2 if you feel like it.

Using MC, pick-up 8 st in a circle at one end of the body. This will be the base for your gills.

Round 1-3: Sc around. This is the tube at the base of the gills – 8 st

The next step is working on the gills.

Ch 6, sl st in each ch down, sl st back into the ring (in the sc at the bottom of the 6 ch). Repeat 8 times all around the tube. You will now have 8 gills. Fasten off and close up the tube using the long tail.

Rhinophores – antennae-like structures – make 2

This part of the amigurumi is worked in the round.

Using CC2, ch 2.

Round 1: Sc 4 in the second chain from the hook (or sc 4 in a magic circle)

Round 2-4: Sc in each st around. Fasten off leaving a long tail for sewing

Base of the body

The start of the base is exactly the same as the start of the body, except that you start with 21 ch rather than 26.

Using MC, ch 21 (main chain + turning chain)

Round 1: Sc in the second ch from the hook, sc 19 (you should now be in your first ch), sc 3 more in your first ch. Sc 19 on the other side of your starting chain, sc 2 more in your last ch – 44 st

Round 2: Sc 19, *2 sc in next st* x2, sc 20, *2 sc in next st* x2, sc 1 – 48 st

Round 3: Sc 19, *2 sc in next st* x4, sc 20, *2 sc in next st* x4, sc 1 – 56 st

Round 4: Sc 20, *2 sc in next st* x6, sc 22, *2 sc in next st* x6, sc 2 – 68 st

Fasten off, leaving a long tail to sew the base to the body.

Assembly

Sew the rhinophores on, at the opposite end from the gills. Then, sew the base on the body, joining to the MC of the body. When there is only a small opening left, stuff the body and finish sewing the base on. You're done!

Dumbo Octopus

size: small

Using medium (worsted) weight yarn and a 3.75 mm (F) crochet hook, your octopus' head should be about 4.5 cm / 1.8" wide. You can easily change the size by using thicker or thinner yarn - just adjust the size of the eyes to match.

SUPPLIES

• medium (worsted) weight yarn

• 3.75mm (F) and 3.5 mm (E) crochet hook

• small amount of stuffing

• 8 mm black beads for eyes (or safety eyes)

• black thread for sewing

• yarn needle and sewing needle

abbreviations:

ch = chain

st = stitch

sts = stitches

sc = single crochet

PATTERN

body:

Work in the round, without joining the rounds. Start with an adjustable ring, or chain 2 and work in the first chain.

With the larger hook:

1. 6 sc in a circle.

2. (2 sc in next st) 6 times. (12 sc)

3. (sc in next st, 2 sc in next st) 6 times. (18 sc)

4. (sc in next st, 2 sc in next st, sc in next st) 6 times. (24 sc)

5-8. sc in each st around, for 4 rounds. (24 sc per round)

9. Working in front loops only, (sc in next st, 2 sc in next st, sc in next st) 8 times. (32 sc)

Go back to working through both loops for the rest of the pattern

10. (sc in next st, 3 sc in next st, sc in next 2 sts) 8 times. (48 sts)

11. (sc in next 2 sts, 5 sc in next st, sc in next 3 sts) 8 times. (80 sts)

Join the last round with a slip stitch. Cut yarn, fasten off, and weave in the yarn tail. At this point, your octopus should look a bit like a sunhat.

ears (make 2):

With the smaller hook, chain 4. Cut yarn, leaving a tail for sewing, and finish off.

The ears are made by sewing both ends of the crochet chain onto the head, forming a very small loop. Sew the ears on top of your amigurumi, between the 2nd and 3rd rounds of the body. Since the body hasn't been stuffed yet, you can knot the ends on the inside to secure the ears in place.

face:

Now you can sew the eyes in place, or attach safety eyes if you're using them. Attach the eyes between the 7th and 8th rounds of the body, about 7 stitches apart. If you want to, add a little mouth by sewing a small, straight stitch in between the eyes.

bottom:

Now make a new piece to close up the bottom of your amigurumi. Start with an adjustable ring, or ch 2 and work in the first chain.

With the smaller hook and a contrasting colour yarn:

1. 6 sc in a circle.

2. (2 sc in next st) 6 times. (12 sc)

3. (sc in next st, 2 sc in next st) 6 times. (18 sc)

4. (sc in next st, 2 sc in next st, sc in next st) 6 times. (24 sc)

Cut yarn, leaving a long tail for sewing, and finish off.

finishing:

Hold your octopus upside-down, and you'll see a little ridge of stitches, formed by working through the front loops in row 9. To close up your amigurumi, start sewing the bottom piece onto this row of stitches.

Before closing tho hole completely, stuff the body so that it's nice and puffy. Sew up the hole, and your octopus is complete!

Puffer Fish

Information

Finished size

Approximately 41/2in (11.5cm) diameter body

Tension

24 sts and 26 rows to 4in (10cm) over double crochet using 3mm hook

Special abbreviation

Picot: The picot appears on the reverse

side of the work. This will be the right side. Insert hook into next st, catch yarn and draw back through stitch (2 loops on hook), (catch yarn and draw through first loop on hook only) 4 times, catch yarn and draw through both loops on hook.

Nelson The Narwhal

SUPPLIES

Worsted weight yarn in the color of your choice

Worsted weight yarn in white or cream

Two (2) 9 mm safety eyes

Small bit of pink yarn for the mouth

Size G (4.0 mm) crochet hook

This pattern is written in standard U.S. crochet terms. Check out www.crochetpatterncentral.com for stitch tutorials.

To increase or decrease the size of the finished product, simply add 1 increase round and 1 "straight around" row, or decrease by the same amount, then do the same for the white belly.

PATTERN

Body:

Round 1: 2 sc, then sc 6 st around. (use a magic circle start if you prefer)

Round 2: 2 sc around (12 st)

Round 3: (1 sc, 2 sc in next stitch) around (18 st)

Round 4:(2 sc, 2 sc in next stitch) around (24 st)

Round 5:(3 sc, 2 sc in next stitch) around (30 st)

Round 6: (4 sc, 2 sc in next stitch) around (36 st)

Round 7: (5 sc, 2 sc in next stitch) around (42 st)

Round 8:(6 sc, 2 sc in next stitch) around (48 st)

Rounds 9-15: sc around (48 st)

Switch to cream colored yarn

Round 16:sc around, back loops only (48 st)

Round 17:(6 sc, dec 1) around (42 st)

Round 18:(5 sc, dec 1) around (36 st)

Round 19:(4 sc, dec 1) around (30 st)

Round 20:(3 sc, dec 1) around (24 st)

Round 21:(2 sc, dec 1) around (18 st)

Attach the eyes at this point in round 14, about 10 stitches apart.

Stuff the body with fiberfill.

Round 22:(1 sc, dec 1) around (12 st)

Round 23:dec around (6 st)

Cut the yarn leaving a long tail. Thread the yarn through a yarn needle and weave through the last stitches. Pull tight and weave in the end.

Fins and tail:

Re-attach the yarn to round 5 in the spot where you changed to the cream yarn. The following is done around the perimeter of the toy.

Sl st 8 stitches, then (sc, hdc, dc, 3 tc, dc, hdc, sc) next stitch

sl st 21 stitches,

then (sc, hdc, dc, 3 tc, dc, hdc, sc),

sl st 7 st,

then (sc, hdc, dc, 5 tc, dc, hdc, sc),

sl st 1,

(sc, hdc, dc, 5 tc, dc, hdc, sc)

sl st around to first fin

Finish off and weave in the ends.

Horn:

Using cream yarn

Round 1: sc 2, then 4 sc in 2nd st. (or use magic ring start)

Round 2: sc around (4 st)

Round 3: (1 sc, 2 sc in next stitch) around (6 st)

Rounds 4-10: sc around (6 st)

Finish off, leaving a long tail for sewing

Attach horn between the eyes of the narwhal

Embroider mouth

Preemie Crochet Squid

SUPPLIES

1 Skein of Red Heart Super Saver Stripes (for 2-3 squids)

Crochet Hook, Size E, 3.5mm (Only one hook size needed)

Crochet Hook, Size F, 3.75mm

Crochet Hook, Size G, 4.0mm

Yarn Needle

Scissors

Pair of Safety Eyes 6mm (optional)

Locking Stitch Markers

Shop my Favorite Tools Here

Stitches and Abbreviations

Ch – Chain

Sc – Single Crochet

Sc2Tog – Single Crochet two Stitches Together

FLO – Front Loop Only

BLO – Back Loop Only

St(s) – Stitches

Slst – Slip Stitch

MC – Magic Circle (Learn a new way to make a MC here!)

Difficulty Level – Easy

Gauge and Finished Size

Gauge

G hook – 5 Sc x 4.5 rows = 1" x 1"

E hook – 6 Sc x 5 rows = 1" x 1"

The Squid using a size G hook is 12.5" long and the squid using the E crochet hook is 10" long.

This preemie crochet squid pattern works up fast and is just adorable. Free crochet pattern for an amigurumi squid by Winding Road Crochet. #squid #crochetsquid #amigurumi #preemiecrochet

Left: Squid made with G hook and longer center tentacles.

Right: Squid made with E hook and shorter center tentacles.

PATTERN

Notes:

Written in US terms.

You will work in continuous rounds. Use a stitch marker to mark the first stitch of each row.

R1: Work 3 Sc into a MC (3)

R2: *Work 2 Sc into the next St* repeat from *to* a total of 3 times. (6)

R3: *Work a Sc into the next St, Work 2 Sc into the next St* repeat from *to* a total of 3 times. (9)

R4: *Work a Sc into the next 2 Sts, Work 2 Sc into the next St* repeat from *to* a total of 3 times. (12)

R5:*Work a Sc into the next 3 Sts, Work 2 Sc into the next St* repeat from *to* a total of 3 times. (15)

R6: *Work a Sc into the next 4 Sts, Work 2 Sc into the next St* repeat from *to* a total of 3 times. (18)

R7: *Work a Sc into the next 5 Sts, Work 2 Sc into the next St* repeat from *to* a total of 3 times. (21)

R8: *Work a Sc into the next 6 Sts, Work 2 Sc into the next St* repeat from *to* a total of 3 times. (24)

R9: Work a Sc into the next 3 Sts, Sk 6 Sts, Work a Sc into the next 6 Sts, Sk 6 Sts, Work a Sc into the last 3 Sts. (12)

Row 9 completed.

R10: *Work a Sc into the next 3 Sts, Work 2 Sc into the next St* repeat from *to* a total of 3 times. (15)

R11: *Work a Sc into the next 4 Sts, Work 2 Sc into the next St* repeat from *to* a total of 3 times. (18)

R12: *Work a Sc into the next 5 Sts, Work 2 Sc into the next St* repeat from *to* a total of 3 times. (21)

R13: *Work a Sc into the next 6 Sts, Work 2 Sc into the next St* repeat from *to* a total of 3 times. (24)

R14: *Work a Sc into the next 7 Sts, Work 2 Sc into the next St* repeat from *to* a total of 3 times. (27)

R15: *Work a Sc into the next 8 Sts, Work 2 Sc into the next St* repeat from *to* a total of 3 times. (30)

R16: *Work a Sc into the next 4 Sts, Work 2 Sc into the next St* repeat from *to* a total of 6 times. (36)

R17-20: Work a Sc into the next 36 Sts. (36)

R21: *Work a Sc into the next 10 Sts, Sc2Tog* repeat from *to* a total of 3 times. (33)

R22: *Work a Sc into the next 9 Sts, Sc2Tog* repeat from *to* a total of 3 times. (30)

R23: *Work a Sc into the next 3 Sts, Sc2Tog* repeat from *to* a total of 6 times. (24)

R24: *Work a Sc into the BLO of the next 2 Sts, Sc2Tog in the BLO* repeat from *to* a total of 6 times. (18)

Note: We will be coming back and working into the front loops of row 24 and row 26.

R25: *Work a Sc into the next St, Sc2Tog* repeat from *to* a total of 6 times. (12)

Note: If you are adding safety eyes or embroidering eyes and a mouth this will be the best time to do it. You can also stuff the squid at this time.

R26: *Sc2Tog in the BLO* repeat from *to* a total of 6 times. (6)

Row 26 complete. Row 24 Front Loops shown.

From where we ended Row 26 we will begin creating tentacles for the squid.

Long Tentacle 1:

Ch 36, Sc in the second chain from the hook, Work a Hdc into the next St, Work a Dc into the next St, Work a Tr into the next 2 Sts, Work a Dc into the next St, Work a Sc into the next 21 Sts. This completed the first tentacle.

Long Tentacle 2:

Slst to one of the FLO of Row 26. Ch36, Sc in the second chain from the hook, Work a Hdc into the next St, Work a Dc into the next St, Work a Tr into the next 2 Sts, Work a Dc into the next St, Work a Sc into the next 21 Sts. This completed the second tentacle.

From here make a loose Slst to on of the FLO of row 24. Here we will start making the curly tentacles.

Loose Slip Stitch from your second long tentacle to the Front Loop of Row 24.

Ch 42, Work a Sc into the second Ch from the hook. Work 2 Sc into the next 40 Sts. Working back into the FLO of row 24, Work a Slst into the FLO of the next 3 Sts repeat from *to* a total of 8 times. Slst to the first curly tentacle and fasten off.

Weave in your ends, wet the long tentacles and pull them a little bit to make them longer than the curly tentacles.

You will have two holes in your squid from where we skipped stitches in row 9. You can sew these up if you like, but I left mine as they were and did not push stuffing that far up the head of the squid. I have provided you a diagram to show you two ways to sew this area.

You can also go back to Row 26 and sew this small hole close, but again I do not think this was necessary.

Use a little yarn or embroidery thread to sew on a mouth if you want a smiling squid.

Amigurumi Seahorse

SUPPLIES

MC: Paintbox Cotton Aran Lime Green or color of choice

C1: Paintbox Cotton Aran Marine Blue or color of choice

F/3.75mm crochet hook

D/3.25mm crochet hook

Cluster fiberfill

6mm safety eyes

scissors

embroidery thread or lightweight yarn in Black

3" length of pipe cleaner

Abbreviations

st(s) – stitch(es)

sl st – slip stitch

sk – skip

ch – chain stitch

sc – single crochet

inc – increase: work 2 sc in same st

dec – decrease: work 2 sc together

FLO – front loop only

Pattern Notes

Rounds in the seahorse are worked continuously with no seams.

Mane is worked in rows and then sewn on to the back of the seahorse.

First few rounds are worked into front loops only to make it easier on those tight rounds. Make sure to not crochet too tightly. You'll need to fit in a pipe cleaner!

Pipe cleaner should have both ends turned in so there's no sharp edges. Final length of pipe cleaner is about 2".

Eyes are placed approximately 1.0-1.25 inches apart.

Amigurumi can be closed using this technique.

Amigurumi Seahorse Instructions

PATTERN

BODY

Worked in continuous rounds.

Worked with MC.

Round 1: Work 6 sc into a magic circle. (6) Secure magic circle right away.

Round 2-6: Work 1 sc into FLO of each st across.

After Round 3, insert pipe cleaner into the tail. Continue working Rounds 4-6 around the pipe cleaner.

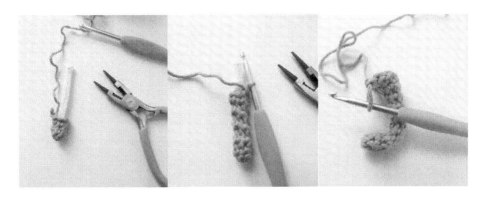

Round 7: Work 1 inc, then 5 sc, all FLO. (7)

Round 8: Work 1 inc, then 6 sc, all FLO. (8)

Round 9: Work 1 inc, then 7 sc, all FLO. (9)

Round 10: Now working through both loops. Work [1 inc, 1 sc] 2x, 1 inc, 4 sc. (12)

Round 11: Work [1 inc, 1 sc] 2x, 1 inc, 7 sc. (15)

Round 12: Work [1 inc, 1 sc] 2x, 1 inc, 10 sc. (18)

Round 13-14: Work 1 sc in each st around. (18)

Round 15: Work [1 sc, dec] 6x around. (12)

Stuff the seahorse up to the neckline.

Round 16: Work [2 sc, dec] 3x around. (9)

Round 17: Work [1 sc, dec] 3x around. (6)

Round 18: Work 2 sc in each st around. (12)

Round 19: Work [1 sc, inc] 6x around. (18)

Round 20: Work [5 sc, inc] 3x around. (21)

Round 21-22: Work 1 sc in each st around. (21)

Round 23: Work [5 sc, dec] 3x around. (18)

Add eyes between Rounds 21 and 22.

Do not sew a mouth.

Round 24: Work [1 sc, dec] 6x around. (12)

Stuff the amigurumi.

Round 25: Work 6 dec. (6)

Fasten off, close, and weave in ends.

SNOUT

Worked with MC and D hook.

Worked in seamed rounds.

Round 1: Work 6 sc into a magic circle. Join to first sc with sl st. (6) Secure magic circle right away.

Round 2: Ch 1. Work 1 sc in BLO of each st around. Join to first sc with sl st. (6)

Fasten off with a length of tail. Tail will be used to sew snout to head.

Sew snout to head centered between the eyes, between Rounds 19-21.

MANE

Worked with C1 and D hook.

Row 1: Ch 17.

Row 2: Work 5 hdc in 3rd ch from hook, sk 1, sl st in next st. *Sk 1, work 5 hdc in next st, sk 1, sl st in next st.* Repeat from * 2 more times for a total of 4 shells.

Fasten off with long tail to sew the mane onto the back of the seahorse.

Mane is situated just along the back of the seahorse's head.

Beginning tail should be woven in.

SIDE FINS

Worked with C1 and D hook.

Row 1: Ch 5.

Row 2: Work 5 hdc in 3rd ch from hook, sk 1, sl st in next st.

Fasten off with tail to sew the side fins to the side of the seahorse, with round side of shell facing forwards.

Beginning tail should be woven in.

Manufactured by Amazon.ca
Bolton, ON

32190347R00042